THE BOY IN THE STRIPED PAJAMAS

by
John Boyne

Teacher Guide

Written by
Linda Herman

Note

The 2007 David Fickling Books paperback edition of the novel, © 2006 by John Boyne, was used to prepare this guide. The page references may differ in other editions. Novel ISBN: 978-0-385-75153-7

Please note: This novel deals with sensitive, mature issues. Parts may contain profanity, sexual references, and/or descriptions of violence. Please assess the appropriateness of this book for the age level and maturity of your students prior to reading and discussing it with them.

ISBN 978-1-56137-838-8

Copyright infringement is a violation of Federal Law.

© 2009 by Novel Units, Inc., Bulverde, Texas. All rights reserved. No part of this publication may be reproduced, translated, stored in a retrieval system, or transmitted in any way or by any means (electronic, mechanical, photocopying, recording, or otherwise) without prior written permission from ECS Learning Systems, Inc.

Photocopying of student worksheets by a classroom teacher at a non-profit school who has purchased this publication for his/her own class is permissible. Reproduction of any part of this publication for an entire school or for a school system, by for-profit institutions and tutoring centers, or for commercial sale is strictly prohibited.

Novel Units is a registered trademark of ECS Learning Systems, Inc.
Printed in the United States of America.

To order, contact your local school supply store, or—

Novel Units, Inc.
P.O. Box 97
Bulverde, TX 78163-0097

Web site: novelunits.com

Table of Contents

Summary 3

About the Author 3

Characters 4

Background Information 5

Initiating Activities 6

Vocabulary Activities 6

Seven Sections 7
    Each section contains: Summary, Vocabulary,
    Discussion Questions, and Supplementary Activities

Post-reading Discussion Questions 21

Post-reading Extension Activities 24

Assessment 25

Scoring Rubric 32

Skills and Strategies

Comprehension
Predicting, cause/effect, plot, summarizing

Literary Elements
Characterization, symbolism, metaphors, similes, conflict, personification, theme, point of view, genre

Vocabulary
Definitions, parts of speech, synonyms/antonyms, target words, idioms

Listening/Speaking
Discussion, performance, presentation, review

Writing
Short story, personal narrative, fable, dialogue, essay, poetry, journal

Thinking
Brainstorming, research, compare/contrast, analysis, problem solving

Across the Curriculum
Social Studies—time line, geography, patriotism, propaganda, the Holocaust, Auschwitz, Adolf Hitler; Science—lice; Math—graphs; Art—design, illustration; Music—appropriate background selections; Current Events—censorship, discrimination

Genre: historical fiction; fable

Setting: 1943–1945; Berlin, Germany and Auschwitz concentration camp, Poland

Themes: friendship, innocence, racism, injustice, denial, duty, empathy

Conflict: person vs. society, person vs. person, person vs. self

Style: narrative

Tone: naïve, apprehensive, serious

Date of First Publication: 2006

Summary

Following a visit from a man called "the Fury," nine-year-old Bruno and his family move from Berlin to a place he calls "Out-With." Bruno does not like his new home and is curious about the people in striped pajamas who live on the other side of the wire fence near his home. Bruno's father is the Commandant of the concentration camp on the other side of the fence, but Father is very secretive about the nature of his work. Bruno understands only that his father is a high-ranking soldier. He is proud and a little fearful of Father. The grim, new setting creates tension in the family, and Bruno becomes very bored and lonely, as living in Out-With isolates him from any interaction with boys his age. One day, Bruno meets Shmuel, a boy in striped pajamas. The two boys discover that their birthday is one of many things they have in common. Sensing that his visits with Shmuel are somehow against the rules, Bruno keeps their friendship a secret from his family. Over the next year, Bruno and Shmuel become best friends, despite the fact that, as Bruno eventually learns from his sister Gretel, the people in striped pajamas are "the opposite" of him. When Bruno's mother decides to return to Berlin with her children, Bruno and Shmuel hatch a plan to go on a "final adventure." With his head shaven due to a recent bout of lice, Bruno puts on a pair of striped pajamas so he can explore Shmuel's side of the fence. He helps Shmuel look for his missing father, but before long, they end up marching with a large crowd of people and are killed in a gas chamber. Bruno's family is puzzled and very troubled by his disappearance. When Father realizes what has happened, his world is shattered and he willingly goes with the Allied soldiers who come to arrest him.

About the Author

John Boyne lives in Dublin, Ireland, where he was born in 1971. At Trinity College in Dublin, he studied English literature, and at the University of East Anglia, Norwich, he studied creative writing. His writing credits include numerous short stories, articles, novellas, and novels. Though he never planned to be a historical novelist, a number of his novels have historical settings. Boyne says he has always loved reading about the past and has been reading Holocaust-related literature since he was a teenager. *The Boy in the Striped Pajamas*, Boyne's fourth novel and first for young readers, has won two Irish Book Awards, the Bisto Book of the Year Award (Ireland), and a Qué Leer Award (Spain), among others. *The Boy in the Striped Pajamas* also topped the *New York Times* Best Sellers List and best sellers lists in many other countries. It has been translated into 38 languages, sold more than 4 million copies, and has been made into a Miramax film of the same name. Boyne's other works include *Crippen*, *Next of Kin*, *The Dare*, and *The House of Special Purpose*.

Characters

Bruno: nine-year-old son of Auschwitz Commandant; naïve and does not understand his father's job; honest; enjoys exploring

Shmuel: Bruno's Jewish friend; has the same birthday as Bruno; lives in the concentration camp

Gretel: Bruno's 12-year-old sister; called a "hopeless case" due to her temperamental nature; know-it-all; copes with unhappiness by rearranging her doll collection

Father (Ralf): Commandant of Out-With camp; an important man for whom the Fury has big plans; patriotic; strict

Mother: proper but caring mother; obedient wife who comes to question her husband's work

Lieutenant Kurt Kotler: 19-year-old soldier; ashamed of his professor father who left Germany in 1938; determined to prove his patriotism; brutal

The Fury: Adolf Hitler; the *Führer* of Germany; meets with Father at the family's house in Berlin

Eva Braun: Adolf Hitler's mistress; friendly to Bruno and Gretel

Maria: family's maid in Berlin and Poland; befriends Bruno

Pavel: Jewish waiter at the Auschwitz house; once a doctor

Herr Liszt: tutor; stresses the importance of the Fatherland's history

Grandfather (Matthias): ran a restaurant in Berlin; nationalist; proud of his son

Grandmother (Nathalie): known for her singing abilities; creative and fun-loving; outspoken and critical of her son's job

Background Information

The following information will enhance students' understanding of the novel.

1. In the aftermath of Germany's loss in World War I, the Nazi Party preached a doctrine of anti-Semitism and promised to restore Germany to greatness. Led by Adolf Hitler, the Nazis blamed the loss of World War I and Germany's subsequent economic troubles on Jews, whom they believed were inferior to Aryans (non-Jewish people of Northern European descent). By 1933, the Nazis had gained enough support that they were able to seize control of Germany's government. On November 9, 1938, German anti-Semitism culminated in a series of riots in which 1,000 synagogues were burned and thousands of Jewish businesses and homes were destroyed. This event is known as *Kristallnacht* ("The Night of Broken Glass") and is generally regarded as the beginning of the Holocaust, a mass "ethnic cleansing" in which the Nazis attempted to eliminate non-Aryans and other groups they viewed as inherently inferior. An estimated six million Jews and an estimated six million non-Jews (homosexuals, Gypsies, non-Jewish Poles, Russian prisoners of war) were eventually executed through various means such as gas chambers, firing squads, and starvation. The bodies were disposed of using crematoria and mass graves. The Nazi invasion of Poland on September 1, 1939, marked the start of World War II. Together with Italy and Japan, they formed the Axis Powers and sought world domination. World War II lasted until 1945, when the Axis Powers were defeated by the Allies (which included such major powers as the United States, France, Britain, and Russia).

2. John Boyne prefers for *The Boy in the Striped Pajamas* to be read in one sitting because, unlike his other works, that is how he wrote the novel. The story of two boys on opposite sides of a Nazi concentration camp fence came to him "fully formed"; "the last two chapters of the book are almost identical, word for word, with the first draft." Boyne prefers the ending to remain a surprise and expressed annoyance when a reviewer revealed how Bruno's story ended. Holocaust experts commend Boyne for attempting the "daunting responsibility" of writing about a difficult topic. However, some experts criticize him for presenting inaccuracies to young readers. Some have noted, for instance, that there were not any unguarded fences in Auschwitz and boys too young to work were immediately put to death. These experts state that the problem is more than a distortion of history, that *The Boy in the Striped Pajamas* gives students the impression that life in the death camps could not have been so awful if Shmuel was able to visit Bruno every day. In interviews, Boyne has admitted that the chance of Bruno and Shmuel's story really happening is unlikely, and that fact, along with the historical liberties taken in the plot's interest, is why the story is presented as a fable.
The story is told from Bruno's point of view, rather than Shmuel's, because Boyne felt it inappropriate for a non-Jewish person to write from the perspective of someone inside the camp. The word "Auschwitz" is not used in the novel because the story is a fable and because genocide, concentration camps, and racial hatred are not confined to the past. Though he would rather readers, especially young readers, find their own lessons in the novel, Boyne ends the novel intentionally stressing people's complacency, then and now.

Initiating Activities

Use one or more of the following to introduce the novel.

1. Brainstorming: Ask students to volunteer definitions of the word *fable*. When they are done, tell students that a fable is a story that teaches a moral lesson and is not based on fact. Have students read the novel's back cover, and then brainstorm as a class what type of fence Bruno may encounter and what moral lesson he and/or the reader may learn.

2. Geography: Instruct students to compare maps of Europe from before and after World War II, and have them review maps showing the locations of Nazi concentration camps (available on the Internet). Students should take special care to note the locations of Berlin and Auschwitz, settings from *The Boy in the Striped Pajamas*.

3. History/Vocabulary: Have students create dictionaries of terms associated with the Nazis (e.g., anti-Semitism, Final Solution, *Führer*, Fatherland, ghetto, propaganda, SS troops, Third Reich).

4. History: Working as a class, have students research the Holocaust and complete the Concept Map on page 26 of this guide.

Vocabulary Activities

1. Vocabulary Squares: Select nine students to sit in three rows of three in the classroom. Give each student a large cutout of an X and an O. Then select two other students: one student is "X," and the other is "O." Student X is asked to define a vocabulary word. S/he must choose one of the nine students sitting in a square to define the word and then state whether s/he agrees or disagrees with the given definition. If Student X correctly agrees or disagrees with the given definition, the sitting student must display an X. If Student X incorrectly agrees or disagrees, the sitting student displays an O. Alternate turns between Students O and X. The first student to have three Xs or Os in a row (vertical, horizontal, or diagonal) is the winner.

2. Twenty Questions: Assign a vocabulary word from the novel to one student. Have the class ask questions of this student to determine the unknown word. Only questions requiring a "yes" or "no" answer may be asked. Encourage the use of questions such as "Is the word a noun?" and "Would a synonym for the word be…?" The student who correctly determines the word is assigned the next vocabulary word.

3. Target Word Definition: Have students create their own definitions for the following vocabulary words: tartan, courgettes, ergo, peckish, boneshaker, and snippets. Encourage students to be creative in their definitions. Read the made-up definitions aloud, and then give the real definitions.

4. Word Sort: Write the following vocabulary words in random order where the class can see them: muster, priorities, reverberated, dominated, forlorn, confirmation, inconsolable, commitment. Have students predict the order in which the words will appear in the novel and justify their predictions. Then write each word's definition beside it, and ask students whether knowing the words' meanings would change their predictions.

Chapters One–Three

Bruno is very unhappy when his family has to move away from Berlin because "the Fury" (the *Führer*, Adolf Hitler) has an important job for Father. The new house, which Bruno is led to believe is called "Out-With" (a distortion of the city name, Auschwitz), is the opposite of Bruno's old home and makes him feel cold and unsafe. Bruno surprises his sister Gretel by showing her the unfriendly children that can be seen from his bedroom window.

Vocabulary
muster
mucky
tartan
spluttering
banister
presumed
desolate
restrictions
courgettes
foreseeable
priorities
greengrocers
commandants

Discussion Questions

1. How would you summarize Bruno's life in Berlin? *(Answers will vary but should include that Bruno's life is comfortable. He enjoys spending time with his friends and his grandparents. Bruno's parents are loving but firm and expect obedience from him and Gretel. The family is wealthy, as shown by their large house and the presence of servants and special visitors.)*

2. What can you infer about Bruno's father from information in Chapter One? *(Bruno's father is an important man, a commandant in the military. Employees report to Father, and he treats Maria as if she is beneath him. He expects obedience from others.)*

3. Why do you think Bruno has difficulties understanding what his father does at work? *(Answers will vary. Suggestions: Bruno is young and naïve. Adults assume he knows things such as who the Fury is. The adults also do not discuss topics with Bruno that they deem unfit for children and intentionally hide what is really happening. For instance, when Bruno asks what Father does, Mother hesitates and only says it is an important job that requires a special man to do it.)*

4. Why would turning all the lights off at night keep Bruno's family safe? What does this tell you about the novel's setting? *(Answers will vary, but it is reasonable to say that darkness may protect people and cities from bombing attacks during wartime because lights let invaders know where people live.)*

5. The new house makes Bruno feel "empty and cold." Why do you think Bruno feels this way? *(Answers will vary. Discussion should include that Bruno moves from a warm, happy home to an isolated house where he senses that adults he trusts [such as Mother and Maria] are no happier than he is.)*

6. Bruno's mother says, "We don't have the luxury of thinking" (p. 13) and "Some people make all the decisions for us" (p. 14). What does Mother mean by this? Is life easier when someone else makes everyone's decisions? *(Answers will vary, but Mother likely means that in wartime it is necessary to act swiftly to ensure one's safety and fulfill one's patriotic duties. The government may place demands upon its citizens to act in what it views as the country's best interests. Bruno's mother feels that her husband, and in effect, she and the rest of the family, are obliged to follow suit. Nevertheless, most people [including Bruno's family] have the ability to think independently and make their own decisions. While having someone make decisions for oneself may be easier, it is important to evaluate situations and reach one's own conclusions, particularly in a time of war, when people's decisions can end up saving or destroying lives.)*

7. What can you infer from Maria's comment that the soldiers "have very serious jobs…or so they think anyway" (p. 19)? *(Answers will vary, but students should infer that Maria doesn't agree with what the soldiers are doing.)*

8. How might the metaphor "civilization of dolls" be important to the story? *(Answers will vary. The dolls seem to represent Gretel's innocence and her controlling nature. Throughout the story, Gretel usually internalizes her unhappiness. Like Bruno, she is upset that the war has upended her former life and fears the chaos she senses around her. She spends hours in her room managing the dolls' mini-world to help her cope with these feelings. For Gretel, this activity seems to nurture an imagined sense of order. Also, the idea of a manipulated civilization may symbolize the Fury's control of the German people.)*

9. In addition to the explanation given by Gretel, how might the name "Out-With" be a pun? *(Answers will vary. "Out-With" may also refer to the Jews' forced relocation and/or their systematic extermination.)*

10. How would you explain Bruno's and Gretel's reactions to the "children" seen from the bedroom window? *(Answers will vary. That Bruno feels "cold and unsafe" and that Gretel is nervous and not "sure she wanted to see these children at all" [p. 28] implies that both children sense something is wrong.)*

11. **Prediction:** Who are the people that live near Bruno's house?

Supplementary Activities

1. Literary Devices: Keep a list of literary devices (such as metaphors, similes, and personification) as you read the novel, citing the page numbers on which you find them. Write one or two sentences explaining the significance of each literary device.

2. Compare/Contrast: Create artwork showing Bruno's old and new houses. Write a paragraph explaining the symbolism of certain differences in them.

3. Comprehension: Bruno likes to say, "We can chalk it up to experience" (p. 14). Think of three existing figures of speech that relate to Bruno's unhappiness with the changes in his life. Then create three figures of speech.

4. Writing: Write about a time that your life changed overnight. Explain how you dealt with the changes.

5. Writing: Write a poem from the point of view of an innocent child.

Chapters Four–Six

Bruno and Gretel wonder who the people behind the fence are. Bruno notices the people all wear striped pajamas. He summons the courage to tell his father that he does not like Out-With. Father insists that his work there is important and sometimes in life a person is not allowed a choice. When Bruno asks him about the people he has seen behind the fence, Father tells him that they are not people. Bruno complains about his father to Maria, but she unexpectedly stands up for Father, explaining how he helped her out of the kindness of his soul. Maria warns Bruno not to say the things he is feeling so the family will remain safe.

Vocabulary
inscription
conviction
efficiency
complementing
clambered
ergo
insolent
irritably
discarding
peckish
reverberated
frenzied

Discussion Questions

1. What clues can you find in Chapter Four that identify what Bruno and Gretel see from the bedroom window? *(Answers will vary. Suggestions: a fence meant to keep people inside; barren ground and simple buildings to economically house many people; smoke stacks for the crematoria; soldiers controlling and abusing the people; work gangs; filthy people who are wounded and crying, wearing striped pajamas like prisoners)*

2. How do you explain Mother's reaction to Maria overhearing her comment, "We should never have let the Fury come to dinner" (p. 40)? *(Answers will vary, but students should infer that Mother, like the other adults, is afraid of being accused of disloyalty to Germany. That Mother ends up shrugging off the incident implies that upon further consideration she realizes she does not care because everything in her life seems to be out of her hands.)*

3. What can you infer from the descriptions of the two trains in Chapter Five? *(Answers will vary but should include that Bruno's train is for regular passengers while the other train is for prisoners. Discussion could cover the circumstances under which prisoners were transported to the Nazi camps.)*

4. What does the scene with Father and the group of five men imply? *(Answers will vary, but the scene demonstrates why Father, with his commanding presence, became Commandant at Out-With, and shows the other men's respect for him. Discussion could cover how Father's joke about his family illustrates Nazis' detachment from their actions and the fact that Nazis lived normal lives while carrying out exterminations.)*

5. What does Father and Bruno's conversation tell you about Father? How would you explain Bruno's willingness to speak freely to, even shout at, his father? *(Answers will vary. Father is undemonstrative and strict, but he loves Bruno, as shown by his taking Bruno's feelings into consideration and allowing him to speak his mind. Father believes he is doing what is best for his family. Bruno speaks out because he wants more than anything to leave Out-With. Though Bruno fears his father at times, his behavior in this situation suggests that Bruno's father has never disciplined him harshly.)*

6. When Bruno asks about the people in the striped pajamas, Father responds, "Those people…well, they're not people at all….at least not as we understand the term…" (p. 53). How does this statement make you feel? *(Answers will vary but should mention that the Nazis' racist beliefs were the Holocaust's impetus. Like other Nazis, Father believes that Jews are subhuman and consequently, feels the exterminations are not something about which he should feel bad.)*

7. Father tells Bruno to "accept the situation in which you find yourself and everything will be so much easier" (p. 53). Why do you think Bruno is dissatisfied with Father's advice? *(Answers will vary, but Bruno's innocence enables him to look at things differently than many adults he knows. His curiosity and love of exploring have made him want to understand things and taught him to ask questions. Bruno wants his family's situation to be better, so it must frustrate him that Father seems to think anything is preferable to proactive behavior. Bruno's father is either too apathetic, hateful, or easily influenced to want to change his life and living situation. Since Bruno is none of these things, he does not understand Father's point of view and sees only a man who is confoundingly unwilling to solve an obvious problem.)*

8. What is the significance of Maria and Bruno's discussion about Father and life at Out-With? *(Maria cannot reconcile the kind man that Father can be with what she knows he is doing in the camp. She is fearful about the current situation and, like Bruno, does not want to be in Out-With; yet she remains loyal to Father. Maria cares about Bruno, as shown by her words of caution and reaction when Bruno counts her as family. Bruno realizes Maria is a person with a history and a life all her own, not just a maid.)*

9. Maria warns Bruno not to say what he really feels because it could cause trouble. What trouble could Bruno's outspokenness bring his family? *(Answers will vary, but if Bruno said something that was deemed unpatriotic, that would reflect badly upon Father. If the Fury thought that Father and his family were traitors, they could be killed.)*

10. **Prediction:** How will Bruno learn to cope with life in Out-With?

Supplementary Activities

1. History: Research the layout of the complex at the Auschwitz-Birkenau concentration camp. Combine information from your findings with descriptions from *The Boy in the Striped Pajamas* to create a map of Bruno's new home. Include a legend that explains your map.

2. History: With your teacher's permission, view a virtual tour of Auschwitz-Birkenau, available at http://www.remember.org/auschwitz (active at time of publication).

3. Vocabulary: An idiom is a phrase that has meaning to people in a particular area of the world but confuses outsiders because the words' joint meaning is often inconsistent with their individual dictionary definitions. "From pillar to post" (p. 33), which Gretel says, is one example of an idiom. Research the meaning of "from pillar to post," and then list idioms from your area.

4. Writing: After watching the people behind the fence, Gretel arranges her dolls. Write a dialogue between Gretel and her dolls in which Gretel discusses her thoughts about Out-With.

5. Brainstorming: After Bruno realizes Maria is a person with her own life, he can guess how she feels being ordered to run Gretel's bath. Empathy is the ability to put yourself in somebody else's shoes, to understand things from his/her viewpoint. Working with a partner, brainstorm ways to show others empathy, and then discuss situations where having this ability would be helpful.

Chapters Seven–Nine

Bruno falls off a swing, and the waiter Pavel, who was once a doctor, cleans his wound. Mother thanks Pavel but says she will tell the Commandant that she cleaned Bruno's wound. Bruno recalls the last time he saw Grandmother, when she was ashamed of Father and his new uniform. Herr Liszt, Bruno and Gretel's new tutor, insists on teaching them the Fatherland's history. Bruno questions whether there are differences between the people living on opposite sides of the fence. He resolves to go exploring along the fence.

Vocabulary

escapade
jumper
appallingly
simpered
woozy
dominated
coincide
tolerant
hysterically
boneshaker

Discussion Questions

1. Why do you think the author includes the story about Franz Roller, the soldier injured in the Great War? *(The scene foreshadows Bruno seeking entertainment so he will not go mad like Herr Roller. The scene tells approximately how long Father has been a soldier and sheds light on Mother's negative view of war and its ravages. Discussion may also cover the long-term effects of war.)*

2. Why does Bruno describe Lieutenant Kotler as "just plain nasty"? *(Lieutenant Kotler believes he is superior to others and flaunts his contempt of those he considers beneath him, especially Pavel [because he is Jewish] and Bruno [because he is young]. Kotler also has "an atmosphere around him that [makes] Bruno feel very cold" [p. 71].)*

3. What is revealed about Pavel in his conversation with Bruno? What does Pavel mean when he says, "I think I've always been here" (p. 84)? *(Pavel's cautious replies to Bruno's questions and his lowly position, despite being a doctor, indicate he is a Jewish prisoner. Pavel is a bright, sensible, gentle person caught in a terrible situation. He may mean that he has always been a victim of discrimination and hence, has always been oppressed. He may also mean that he has been in Auschwitz so long and been tortured so much that he does not remember humane treatment.)*

4. Why might Mother thanking Pavel for cleaning Bruno's wound be important? Why do you think Mother wants to take credit? *(Answers will vary. If Mother understands and appreciates what Pavel has done for Bruno, this greatly decreases the chances that Pavel will get in trouble. In addition, it is possible that Mother may be seeing Pavel as a kind person, rather than as a prisoner, for the first time. The Commandant may not want a Jew touching or interacting with his son, and/or he may not want to be indebted to a prisoner. Mother taking credit ensures Pavel's protection from any accusations of wrongdoing relating to the incident.)*

5. What does Grandmother mean when she says, "dressing up like a puppet on a string" (p. 90)? *(Answers will vary. Grandmother is accusing her son and the German military of allowing the Fury to manipulate their every move, as if they cannot think for themselves. The quote also implies that Father does not care about the nature of his position, so long as it garners people's special attention.)*

6. Compare and contrast Grandfather's and Grandmother's opinions of Father's new commandant position and uniform. Why do you think their opinions differ? *(Grandfather is proud of his son's promotion and believes his son is helping Germany reclaim its pride and correct wrongs that have been done. Grandmother is ashamed. She sees the terrible things the Nazis are doing and is upset that Father's new position and uniform represent those things. Answers will vary. Suggestions: Like Father, Grandfather believes it is patriotic to unquestioningly support Germany's Nazi government. He chooses only to see that the Nazis have made Germany powerful. Grandmother puts her innate sense of right and wrong before her respect for her country's government. Grandmother knows that living according to one's conscience is the only way to truly honor one's country.)*

7. What subject is Herr Liszt mainly interested in teaching? Why? *(He is mainly interested in teaching the history of the Fatherland, including the "great wrongs" done to the German people. Answers will vary. Herr Liszt wants to teach Nazi propaganda. That is, through his distorted account of history, he wants to stir in Bruno a great sense of righteous indignation and a need for vengeance. He believes the Jews are the cause of Germany's problems and wants Aryan Germans to grow up to be Nazis.)*

8. Why do you think Bruno never really wondered about the circumstances behind the fence? What causes him to question whether there are any differences between the people living on both sides of the fence? *(Answers will vary. Since the adults do not discuss the camp in his presence and since Bruno is usually preoccupied with his unhappiness in Out-With, he has not really thought about what happens in the camp until now. Bruno's father would have him believe that he has nothing in common with the people on the other side of the fence. However, Bruno's boredom, loneliness, innocence, and curious nature make him open-minded and interested to learn what he can about this mysteriously segregated population of people.)*

9. **Prediction:** What will Bruno find while exploring?

Supplementary Activities

1. Comprehension: Bruno does not understand what Pavel means when he says, "Just because a man glances up at the sky at night does not make him an astronomer, you know" (p. 82). Write a paragraph or two that explains what you think Pavel is saying.

2. Drama: Working with classmates, write and stage a play related to Germany. Include songs, dances, and magic tricks. At the end of your play, recite a famous German poem.

3. History: Draw an illustration of Father's uniform. Use information from the novel and independent research for details about the uniforms and decorations worn by Nazi officers. Write a summary explaining the significance of the uniforms' various parts.

4. History/Speaking: One part of the Nazi propaganda campaign was a movement to control which books people could read. The Nazis burned 25,000 books on May 10, 1933, including works by authors such as Albert Einstein, Ernest Hemingway, and Helen Keller. Find a current news story about censorship, and summarize the article in class.

Chapters Ten–Twelve

While exploring, Bruno meets Shmuel, a boy who lives behind the fence, and learns Out-With is in Poland. Bruno asks about the people on Shmuel's side of the fence. The story flashes back to months earlier when Hitler and Eva Braun visited Bruno's parents and plans were made for Bruno's family to move to Out-With. Shmuel recounts how he was forced to live in the horrible conditions in the Out-With camp. Bruno does not believe everything Shmuel says and makes naïve comparisons to his own life. He keeps his friendship with Shmuel a secret from his family.

Vocabulary

despair
forlorn
confirmation
crockery
extravagant
enunciating
ushered
disdain
snippets
contradict

Discussion Questions

1. Bruno thinks Shmuel's name "sounds like the wind blowing" (p. 108). Shmuel thinks Bruno's name "sounds like someone who's rubbing their arms to keep warm" (p. 109). What can you infer from the simile each boy uses? *(Answers will vary, but the boys' impressions of each other's names reflect their circumstances. Bruno's simile implies freedom, while Shmuel's simile pertains to survival.)*

2. Why do you think Shmuel remains quiet when Bruno states that Germany is superior? *(Answers will vary, but it is reasonable to say that Shmuel does not want to fight with a new friend. He is probably also hesitant to speak against Germans since the soldiers controlling the camp are German.)*

3. Why do you think Chapter Eleven, titled "The Fury," is inserted into the middle of the story? Why didn't the author start the story with this chapter? *(Answers will vary. The chapter provides readers vital clues regarding setting and characters, but by withholding the details of the Fury's visit until this point, the author is better able to pull readers into the story and build suspense. Without the details about the visit, the author is able to repeatedly hint at the horrific nature of Father's work without concretely establishing what that work is. Most readers will know what Father does prior to Chapter Eleven, but the more subtle hints the reader periodically receives until Chapter Eleven create the sense of a disturbing, looming hidden truth. Also, while the story is told in third person, the reader essentially sees things from Bruno's point of view. Bruno is naïve, so there is naturally a correlation between Bruno's sense of what details are most pertinent to the story and the order in which the reader receives certain pieces of information.)*

4. How is "the Fury" a pun? *(Answers will vary. Suggestions: "Fury" sounds like "führer," the German word for leader. Hitler was an angry, hateful person, and his speeches stirred a fury in Aryan Germans that resulted in the Holocaust.)*

5. What important clues are included in the partial conversation Bruno overhears between his parents about leaving Berlin? *(The family is moving to an undesirable place. Mother is aware something unnatural and distasteful occurs at this place, though the Fury and/or Father does not agree. Father decides to follow orders since he is unwilling to risk facing unpleasant consequences. Mother does not want the children anywhere near the concentration camp.)*

6. Compare and contrast Bruno's and Shmuel's situations. Do you agree with Bruno that Shmuel's story isn't such a terrible thing? Why does Bruno feel the way he does? *(Both boys are taken from their homes and end up at Out-With. However, Bruno's trip was pleasant and he has most of the comforts of home; Shmuel's trip was miserable, he is in a prison, and his mother was taken away. Answers will vary, but Bruno does not realize the seriousness of Shmuel's situation because he has lived a sheltered life, as shown by his inability to believe parts of Shmuel's story.)*

7. Why is Bruno unsure that inviting Shmuel to dinner is a good idea? *(Answers will vary. Though Bruno does not understand what is happening behind the fence, he knows his parents think the people on the other side are different. Bruno knows that adults establish and maintain the orders and rules in place in the world, so he probably guesses that these orders and rules are in place for a reason that is obvious and important to adults and that transgressing them would have consequences of some kind.)*

8. Why do Bruno and Shmuel become friends? Do you think they would be friends if they had met in Berlin? *(Answers will vary. The boys' loneliness and unhappiness with the changes in their lives brings them together. On the one hand, one might say that they would be friends if they met in Berlin since they seem to get along well. However, both boys were happy enough in their former lives that if their lives had continued on in the ways to which they were accustomed, they might not have been actively seeking new friends.)*

9. **Prediction:** Will Bruno keep his friendship with Shmuel a secret?

Supplementary Activities

1. Writing: Bruno tells Shmuel that "…Germany is the greatest of all countries…. We're superior" (p. 112). Write an essay explaining the differences between patriotism and nationalism. Give examples from the novel and other sources to support your answers.

2. History: Research Adolf Hitler's rise to power. Create an illustrated time line of important facts and dates. Include information about his childhood.

3. History: Research the history of the Star of David or the swastika. Share your findings in class.

4. Geography: Working in small groups, find photos and maps of Jewish ghettos (available on the Internet). Research the purposes for ghettos. Create a multimedia presentation for the class.

Chapters Thirteen–Fourteen

Bruno meets Shmuel most every day and begins bringing him food, but Bruno still does not understand what is happening to the people behind the fence. At dinner, it becomes obvious that Pavel is slowly dying, as he is beginning to make errors, such as when he spills wine on Lieutenant Kotler, who becomes extremely angry with Pavel. Bruno cannot understand why no one intervenes, but the incident helps him realize that at Out-With he must always behave (or at least give the appearance of doing so). Bruno accidentally mentions Shmuel to Gretel but quickly covers by saying Shmuel is his imaginary friend. Bruno realizes he did not support Shmuel emotionally when his friend told him about the disappearances of people behind the fence, including Shmuel's grandfather.

Vocabulary

catastrophe
vital
revival
tubercular
ginger
dilemma
crucial
undeniable
sarcasm
sophistication
flounced

Discussion Questions

1. Before Maria tells Bruno why Pavel is no longer a doctor, she says, "…you mustn't tell anyone—do you understand? We would all get in terrible trouble" (p. 137). Why might knowing about Pavel's life get Bruno or Maria in trouble? *(Answers will vary. Bruno and Maria are discussing why a skilled person would be used as a servant. It is in the Nazis' best interest if people simply accept political propaganda since the reasons for their actions are irrational and motivated by hate. Those who question what is happening threaten the Nazis' grand scheme.)*

2. How does Bruno react when he doesn't understand or like Shmuel's comments? Why do you think Bruno reacts as he does? *(When Shmuel's comments make Bruno irritable, Bruno nods as if he understands or pretends he does not hear and changes the subject, as shown when Shmuel comments that the soldiers do not want people to get better and when Shmuel says Bruno does not understand what it is like on Shmuel's side of the fence. Sometimes Bruno just remains quiet to avoid an argument, as shown when Shmuel refuses to say that Father is a good soldier. Answers will vary, but Bruno likely acts as he does because he wants to keep Shmuel as a friend. Hearing bad things about Father makes Bruno angry and may raise questions about his father that Bruno is not ready to face. When problems or ethical questions arise, Bruno's family generally chooses to ignore them, and it is possible that Bruno has subconsciously adopted this harmful behavior.)*

3. What is significant about Bruno noticing changes in Pavel? *(Answers will vary. Bruno now thinks of Pavel as a person instead of a waiter and realizes that Pavel is slowly dying. This realization is significant because it shows Bruno's developing sense of empathy for the prisoners.)*

4. What does Father mean when he says, "…it's history that's got us here today….We are correcting history here" (pp. 143–144)? *(Answers will vary. Like other Nazis, Father likely believes that Jews were responsible for Germany's defeat in World War I and Germany's subsequent economic problems. He also probably thinks that true Germans are Aryans and that Jews' presence can only dilute "pure" German blood and hinder the country's progress. The Nazi reasoning is that only the strongest [Aryans] should survive and the only reason that "weaker" races or individuals exist in the first place is because compassion has stood in the way of the natural selection process for so long. "Purifying" the human race and conquering other countries was the Nazis' attempt to give Germany the present and future for which they believed it was always destined.)*

5. Why does Father question Lieutenant Kotler about his father, the professor? *(Father questions the professor's loyalty to Germany and thinks anyone not participating in Germany's "national revival" must be a traitor or a coward. Father's questioning appears to be an intentional attempt to intimidate Lieutenant Kotler, seemingly for personal reasons.)*

6. What is significant about Lieutenant Kotler's father leaving Germany in 1938? *(This is the year that Germany invaded Austria. This act marked the beginning of Germany's "expansion," and leaving Germany at this time would seem to indicate that one opposed the new Nazi policies.)*

7. How does Kotler's treatment of Pavel affect Bruno? What is significant about Bruno's reaction? *(He seems finally to realize that something wrong is happening at Out-With. Bruno's compassion again shows his developing empathy and serves to highlight the callousness of those around him, who seem unconcerned about Pavel's fate.)*

8. What does Bruno realize when he tells Gretel about his "imaginary friend"? *(He realizes that he did not understand how sad Shmuel was about his missing friends and grandfather and failed to comfort him; he sees that he owes Shmuel an apology.)*

9. **Prediction:** Who else will disappear from Out-With?

Supplementary Activities

1. History/Math: Create a graph to show the number of Holocaust victims, both Jewish and non-Jewish. Include statistics for camps, ghettos, Security Police, and other nonmilitary-related deaths. Write a note to accompany your graph that explains why some sources' facts differ (e.g., record-keeping, "Holocaust deniers").

2. Writing: Imagine you are an advice columnist like "Dear Abby" and that the following letter will be printed in your newspaper column. Write a response to be published with the letter.

    "Dear _____,

    My father is generally a kind and thoughtful man, yet he didn't stop Lieutenant Kotler from getting angry at Pavel, our waiter. My friend Shmuel says there aren't any good soldiers and that includes my father, who is the Commandant. How can my father be a kind man and allow awful things to happen? Signed, Bruno."

3. Writing: Write about a time you or someone you know had a friendship that contradicted stereotypes.

Chapters Fifteen–Seventeen

Bruno discovers Shmuel in the kitchen polishing glasses for an officers' party. Lieutenant Kotler terrifies both boys when he catches them talking, and Bruno denies knowing Shmuel. A week later, Bruno apologizes to Shmuel, who forgives him and lifts up the fence to shake hands—the first time the two boys touch. Bruno learns from Gretel that the fence exists to keep Jews inside and that he and Gretel are "the opposite" of Jews. When Mother discovers that Bruno has lice, Father shaves Bruno's head, making Bruno look like a healthy version of Shmuel. Mother and Father argue about Father's work and decide that Mother, Gretel, and Bruno will return to Berlin. Bruno, who is now happy at Out-With, dreads telling Shmuel that he is leaving.

Vocabulary

anatomy
grimaced
inconsolable
persisted
misshapen
dwindling
commitment
indirect
exasperated
revealed

Discussion Questions

1. How does Bruno react when Shmuel shows him his bony fingers and says, "Everyone on my side of the fence looks like this now" (p. 168)? Why do you think Bruno still does not understand what is happening at Out-With? *(Bruno wonders if what is going on at Out-With is a very bad idea because it makes people look so unhealthy. Answers will vary. Suggestions: Bruno is too innocent to realize Shmuel and others are starving or even what "starving" really means. He has never had to do without life's necessities and comforts.)*

2. Why does Bruno deny knowing Shmuel? What would Lieutenant Kotler have done if Bruno had told the truth? *(Answers will vary but should include discussion of how fear can make people behave in unpredictable ways. Had Bruno told the truth, Kotler would probably have gotten angry with both boys and notified Bruno's father of what happened. Unless the boys were able to convince someone that they had only just met, extreme measures would have been taken to make sure they never saw each other again.)*

3. What is significant about how Shmuel forgives Bruno? *(Shmuel shaking Bruno's hand is the first time the boys touch. Discussion could also cover how quickly and sincerely Shmuel forgives Bruno, showing Shmuel's remarkable kindness despite the horrors to which he is routinely subjected.)*

4. What causes Bruno to come to think of Out-With as home? Do you think Out-With is really no longer "empty and cold" with "nothing to be happy about" (p. 13) as Bruno first thought? *(Bruno has Shmuel as a friend and is forgetting his friends in Berlin. He accepts the differences between Out-With and Berlin and realizes he has much to be happy about. Out-With is the same or worse than ever, but the warmth of friendship affects Bruno's viewpoint. This comfort, Bruno's naïveté, and his inability to accept that his father is an integral part of something evil mean that Bruno does not perceive the horror on the other side of the fence.)*

5. Why do you think Lieutenant Kotler is transferred from Out-With? *(Answers will vary. Though it is possible that Father has found out something about Kotler's father, it is more likely that Father has discovered the affair between Kotler and Mother. Note the references to Kotler whispering to Mother, Mother laughing at Kotler's jokes more than Father's, and Mother calling Kotler "precious" before spending time alone with him.)*

6. Bruno is "pleased to see that [Shmuel] seemed a lot happier these days" (p. 178). Why do you think Shmuel is happier? *(Answers will vary, but Shmuel enjoys his friendship with Bruno, and he must be relieved that Lieutenant Kotler is gone.)*

7. How does Gretel form her opinion of the people on the fence's other side? What can you infer from her comments about Jews and "Opposites"? *(Answers will vary. Father, Herr Liszt, Lieutenant Kotler, or newspaper reports are the most likely sources of Gretel's information, which extends no farther than that she and Bruno are the opposite of Jews and that they are not supposed to like Jews. She is unable to explain these beliefs and is clearly just repeating someone else's opinion. Gretel is young and impressionable. Since the information probably came from someone she respects, she was willing to accept the bigoted beliefs without an explanation. Doing so also probably helped her make sense of the living situation at Out-With, which seems to have been troubling and confusing her for some time now.)*

8. What is the significance of Bruno's haircut? *(Bruno's head is shaved because he has lice. After this haircut he looks a lot like Shmuel. Lice was a common problem in concentration camps, and the strong resemblance between the two boys after Bruno's haircut is meant to show that prejudice senselessly divides human beings.)*

9. Father comes to realize that Out-With is not a place to raise children. How do you think Father would react if Gretel and Bruno really knew what happens behind the fence? *(Answers will vary, but Father's reactions might include a discussion about shame, the duties of a soldier, or Nazi beliefs.)*

10. **Prediction:** How will Shmuel react to the news of Bruno's upcoming return to Berlin?

Supplementary Activities

1. Comprehension: Rewrite the scene in Bruno's kitchen from Shmuel's point of view. Use the five senses in your writing.

2. Art: Bruno notices differences between his hand and Shmuel's. Create a photo essay or other artistic impression that compares and contrasts the lives of people on both sides of the fence.

3. Science: Chart the life cycle of head lice. Include a list of interesting facts about lice with your chart.

4. Current Events: Divide a sheet of paper into two columns. In the left column, list examples of prejudice happening today. In the right column, list ways to prevent such incidents from occurring.

Chapters Eighteen–Twenty

Bruno and Shmuel plan a final adventure where Bruno will explore the other side of the fence and help look for Shmuel's missing father. Bruno puts on the striped pajamas Shmuel brings him and remembers Grandmother saying, "You wear the right outfit and you feel like the person you're pretending to be" (p. 205). On the other side of the fence, instead of seeing the happy families he expected to find, Bruno sees miserable people and laughing soldiers. He and Shmuel are caught in a crowd of people and forced to march into what turns out to be a gas chamber. In the ensuing chaos, Bruno clings to his best friend's hand. Bruno's family never sees him again. Father eventually realizes what happened to Bruno and is destroyed by the knowledge. Bruno's story ends with the line: "…nothing like that could ever happen again. Not in this day and age" (p. 216).

Vocabulary
coincidences
squelched
implanted
despatch
prospect
random
disturbance
mercilessly

Discussion Questions

1. After his talk with Gretel about the purpose of the fence, why do you think Bruno still doesn't believe the soldiers could hate Shmuel and the other Jews? *(Answers will vary, but the truth is too horrible for Bruno to comprehend. Bruno thinks of Father and the soldiers as he knows them at the house because that is his experience with them and because believing Shmuel implicates Father.)*

2. Do you think Shmuel believes he might someday go on a holiday to Berlin? *(Answers will vary. Shmuel does not fully understand what is happening at the camp and why people are disappearing, but the camp's hostile environment has certainly planted doubts in his mind about what the future might hold. When Bruno suggests that he will one day visit Berlin, his affirmative reply is less than confident.)*

3. What do the "happy, laughing, shouting soldiers" (p. 208) indicate about the other side of the fence? *(The soldiers hate the Jews and enjoy humiliating them.)*

4. What do you think would have happened if Bruno had told the crowd that his father was the Commandant? *(Answers will vary. Even if someone paid attention to him amidst the chaos before the gassing, it is unlikely that anyone would have believed him. His features are apparently not exclusive to his true ethnicity, and the extraordinary story of his friendship with Shmuel and entry into the camp would probably strike most as a desperate attempt to escape execution.)*

5. What happens to Bruno and Shmuel? *(Students should infer that the boys died in a gas chamber.)*

6. Father once asked Bruno, "Do you think that I would have made such a success of my life if I hadn't learned when to argue and when to keep my mouth shut and follow orders" (p. 49)? Explain whether you think Father considers his life a success at the end of the story. *(Answers will vary, but Father's actions—e.g., ordering soldiers around mercilessly until they dislike him, collapsing when he realizes what happened to Bruno, not minding that the Allied soldiers take him away or what they might do to him—imply that, at the very least, Father knows he has severely failed as a parent. It is also possible that Father realizes he is guilty of mass murder and has done nothing to better his country.)*

7. Where do you think the soldiers took Father? *(Answers will vary, but Allied soldiers would have taken him to be tried for crimes against humanity, for which he would almost certainly be convicted and executed.)*

8. Why does the author end the story by saying, "Of course all this happened a long time ago and nothing like that could ever happen again. Not in this day and age" (p. 216)? *(Answers will vary. The author knows that for many people it is easy and more comfortable to consign genocide to the past. He wants to stress that atrocities are happening today so that people will take action to help the victims.)*

Supplementary Activities

1. Comprehension: Divide the class into eight teams. Each team should choose one of the questions found in the Reader's Guide at the end of the novel (Note: These questions may not be included in some editions of the novel.). Teams should then prepare answers to their questions and share them with the class.
2. Comprehension: Complete the Sequencing Events chart on page 27 of this guide.
3. Character Analysis: Complete the Sorting Characters chart on page 28 of this guide. On a separate sheet of paper, make a list of the novel's themes.

Post-reading Discussion Questions

1. Were you surprised by the ending of the story? How did it make you feel? *(Answers will vary.)*

2. Do you like that the story is told from Bruno's point of view? How does using this viewpoint affect the storytelling process and the reader's involvement in the story? *(Answers will vary. Due to Bruno's naïveté, certain information is left out or only partially explained. The reader is left to fill in the blanks. This gets the reader actively involved in the novel and enriches the story's emotional resonance. Using Bruno's viewpoint distances readers from the details of the atrocities committed in Auschwitz but through repeated implication captures the sense that something shocking and horrifying is occurring in the city. In addition, Bruno's misinterpretations add comic relief to the story, as shown when he questions whether Pavel is a good doctor since he must "practice." If the story had been told from Father's point of view, there would be little suspense or humor and readers would probably focus more on their anger with Father and less on their attachment to the story's protagonists, Bruno and Shmuel.)*

3. What do you think is the author's main message? What other main themes did you find? *(Answers will vary. The author wants readers to realize the senselessness of prejudice and take action against genocide; Some themes include the gift of friendship, innocence vs. experience, racism's destructive power, the value of empathy, the positive and negative effects of loyalty, the problem of injustice, moral isolation, and emotional isolation.)*

4. Some reviewers have been critical of the novel, noting its various historical inaccuracies. For example, in reality, Bruno would have already been part of the *Pimpfen* (the Nazi club for young boys) for four years and been taught some Nazi beliefs. John Boyne has been quoted as saying that for his other novels he did considerable research, but for this novel he simply sat down and wrote the story that was in his head. Why do you think Boyne wrote the novel this way? Explain whether you think the novel is a worthwhile read regardless of its historical inaccuracies. *(Answers will vary, but Boyne likely felt that the story's important message would be compromised if he focused on historical accuracy. In Bruno, Boyne gives the average reader a character not dissimilar from his/her nine-year-old self. If Bruno were, for example, part of the Pimpfen, he would be hard for readers to relate to and a friendship with Shmuel would be very implausible. By framing his story as a fable, a form whose primary purpose is to teach a lesson, Boyne gains the artistic freedom to make Bruno a more typical nine-year-old. In doing so, Boyne is able to ask, "What if...?" and put his message, the senselessness of prejudice, at the forefront.)*

5. Do you feel, as some of Boyne's critics do, that *The Boy in the Striped Pajamas* makes life in a concentration camp seem tolerable? *(Answers will vary. However, it is reasonable to say that since the story alludes to the starvation, abuse, cramped and dirty living quarters, and mass exterminations [one of which claims the lives of the story's protagonists] that were routine for Jews at Auschwitz, there is little to suggest that concentration camp life was anything but nightmarish.)*

6. What kind of person is Bruno's mother, and in what ways is Gretel similar to her? What might these characters symbolize, and what might Boyne be trying to say through them? *(Mother is a loving parent and is depressed by the environment at Out-With. She seems to know what is right but fails to take a grand stand against evil the way Grandmother, in her place, likely would have. She objects to the move and to her children being raised at Out-With. Her relationship with Father deteriorates, she is outraged when Father calls what he does work, and she states that Grandmother would "turn in her grave" [p. 177] if she knew that the Fury had sent a wreath to her funeral. Faced with the great moral dilemma of being married to a Nazi and living next door to a place where mass killings are taking place, beyond her vocal protests and her one effort to protect Pavel, her response is limited to drinking sherry, napping, and having an affair with a younger Nazi. When Mother is faced with great evil, she usually turns inward and takes care of herself or, as she*

does near the end of the story, her children. It is noteworthy that her real name is never given. She fails to distinguish herself as anything other than a caring mother. Like her mother, in the hostile atmosphere of Out-With, Gretel too turns inward. Mother makes herself feel better by manipulating and reshaping her own little world by drinking or having an exciting liaison with a younger man. Gretel deals with her emotional turmoil by quietly spending hours alone manipulating her little doll world. Indeed, it seems that Gretel has learned much from her mother's example; she too finds Lieutenant Kotler a welcome distraction. Both characters remain emotionally isolated and are primarily concerned with tending to their own needs. Gretel and Mother likely symbolize the selfish German citizens who were so concerned with maintaining their own sense of emotional well-being that in their emotional isolation they failed to fulfill their moral responsibilities. Through Mother and Gretel, Boyne may mean to imply that emotional isolation leads to moral isolation, which allows civilization's destruction.)

7. How is it possible that Bruno's father was both a good parent and a murderous Nazi? *(Answers will vary, but note that Rudolf Hoess, Auschwitz's Commandant from 1940 to 1943, was also a dedicated family man. Hoess stated that in his life, love of country and family were the guiding principles behind his actions. Hoess had a conscience, but he was taught to and chose to ignore it, believing that it was a weakness that would stand in the way of the Nazi ideology in which he placed so much faith. Father, too, probably compartmentalized actions he felt were wrong as necessary personal sacrifices for what he viewed as the betterment of his race and country. In the days leading up to his execution, Hoess realized the great evil for which he was responsible and wrote to his eldest son, "Keep your good heart. Become a person who lets himself be guided primarily by warmth and humanity. Learn to think and judge for yourself, responsibly. Don't accept everything without criticism and as absolutely true....The biggest mistake of my life was that I believed everything faithfully which came from the top, and I didn't dare to have the least bit of doubt about the truth of that which was presented to me....In all your undertakings, don't just let your mind speak, but listen above all to the voice in your heart" [http://theology.shu.edu/lectures/massmurder.htm, active at time of publication].)*

8. How is Bruno's desire to explore important to the story? *(Answers will vary, but Bruno's desire to explore his world is what pushes the plot forward. Though some might argue that Bruno could have met Shmuel for the first time at the house prior to the officers' party, it is unlikely that Bruno would have actively pursued such a potentially risky friendship [and venture to the fence's other side] without the curiosity with which Boyne imbued him.)*

9. How would the story be different if Bruno had not kept Shmuel a secret from his family? *(Answers will vary. Bruno would have been forbidden to meet Shmuel. He would never have had important positive experiences with a Jewish person and would not have entered the concentration camp. It is even possible that in light of his upbringing and the bitterness that could result from Germany's defeat and/or his father's arrest, Bruno could have grown up to be a racist.)*

10. What do you think the fence represents? How is it important to the novel? *(Answers will vary. The fence physically separates Aryans and Jews, creating an "us versus them" situation. On first glance, it seems only to represent confinement, evil, control, intimidation, fear, and humiliation. The novel encourages readers to look for such fences in real life. On the other hand, the fence ultimately serves to illustrate the human race's indivisibility. The fence initially succeeds in isolating both boys from normal social interaction. However, since fences are unnatural and man-made [like the prejudices that motivate their construction in the first place] and humans are social creatures by nature, there is no such thing as a fool-proof fence. A fence's greatest strength as a tool of division [that it has two sides] is, paradoxically, also its greatest weakness. For each side of the fence there is a person or group of people, and each person or group of people will, by their own nature, be drawn to that fence in the hope of communicating with those on the other side. Because of the fence, both boys are starved for normal social interaction with non-family members. This need for normal social interaction eventually*

brings the boys together at the point of division, the fence. They cannot interact in any physical way, so they spend all of their time talking, getting to know one another. The result is that each boy realizes he has much in common with the person on the other side of the fence. So in this way, the fence ends up doing the opposite of what it was meant to do and indirectly unites Jews and Aryans. In this way, the fence illustrates that indiscriminate unity is humanity's natural state.)

11. Do you think you will look at other historical events from multiple points of view after reading this novel? What advantages might there be to doing this? *(Answers will vary. Attempting to look at historical events from different points of view can help one better understand the motivations behind and effects of people's actions. Learning from history in this way can help ensure that people generally aspire to acts that truly contribute to society's greater good.)*

12. Some book reviewers do not think *The Boy in the Striped Pajamas* is a novel for young readers. In an interview, the author said, "There are layers of the story for both children and adults to explore." Discuss the "layers" you found in the story. What is the youngest age group you think should read the novel? *(Answers will vary. Examples of "layers" include the concentration camp's purpose, the double meanings found in Boyle's puns, the bits of adults' conversations Bruno overhears, the relationship between Lieutenant Kotler and Mother, and Gretel's gradual indoctrination into Nazi propaganda.)*

Post-reading Extension Activities

Writing

1. Write a modern-day fable that teaches a moral lesson about innocence and/or prejudice.
2. Write a poem about the relationship between Bruno and Shmuel. How did their friendship grow? Include imagery from the novel.
3. Write a story where duty and obedience conflict with human rights.

Listening/Speaking

4. View the movie *Schindler's List*. Discuss in class what you learn about concentration camps that *The Boy in the Striped Pajamas* did not tell you.
5. Find a current news story that relates to *The Boy in the Striped Pajamas*. The story can relate to a theme, place, event, or group of people characterized in the novel. Prepare an oral report that summarizes the article and how it relates to the novel.

Drama/Music

6. Write and stage a play that includes the use of puns.
7. Compose a song about a character in the novel. Pair your lyrics with the tune of one of your favorite songs.
8. Working with a small group, write and stage a scene from the novel. Add appropriate background music and lighting.

Art

9. Design a poster advertising the novel.
10. Using any medium, show events from the story that change how Bruno views people.

Research

11. Choose "Art in Auschwitz" or "Music of the Holocaust" as a topic. Write a report about several works of art or musical compositions and their importance to history.
12. Research propaganda techniques, and write a report in which you compare and contrast American and Nazi propaganda posters from the same time period.
13. Prepare a time line that tells the history of the Auschwitz-Birkenau concentration camp.
14. Write a biography of Rudolf Hoess, focusing on the motives for his crimes against humanity and his change of heart shortly before his execution.

Assessment for *The Boy in the Striped Pajamas*

Assessment is an ongoing process. The following ten items can be completed during study of the novel. Once finished, the student and teacher will check the work. Points may be added to indicate the level of understanding.

Name _____ Date _____

Student	Teacher	
_____	_____	1. Keep a literary journal as you read the novel, noting themes, symbols, important events, and your impressions.
_____	_____	2. Complete the Story Map on page 29 of this guide.
_____	_____	3. Using at least ten vocabulary words, write a summary of the novel.
_____	_____	4. Complete the Character Web on page 30 of this guide. On a separate sheet of paper, write a paragraph that explains whether the character you chose learns any lessons.
_____	_____	5. Write three review questions, and use these to participate in an oral review.
_____	_____	6. Complete the Cause/Effect chart on page 31 of this guide.
_____	_____	7. Choose a theme from the novel, and explain to the class how it is developed.
_____	_____	8. Complete at least two Post-reading Extension Activities, and present one to the class.
_____	_____	9. Working in a small group, share your completed vocabulary, comprehension, character analysis, and literary analysis activities.
_____	_____	10. Correct all quizzes or tests taken over the novel.

Concept Map

Directions: Research the Holocaust, and complete the map below.

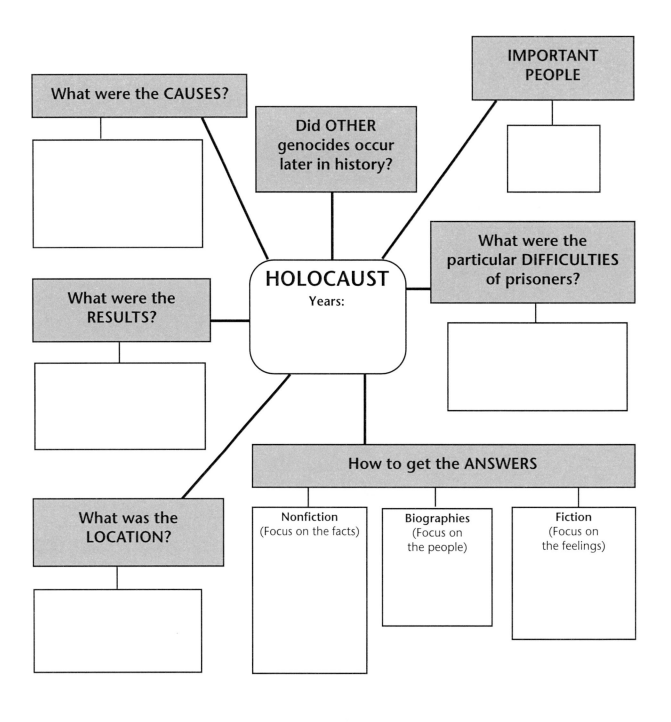

Sequencing Events

Directions: In the boxes below, illustrate main events throughout the story in the order they occurred. Write an explanation for each illustration on the corresponding line below the boxes.

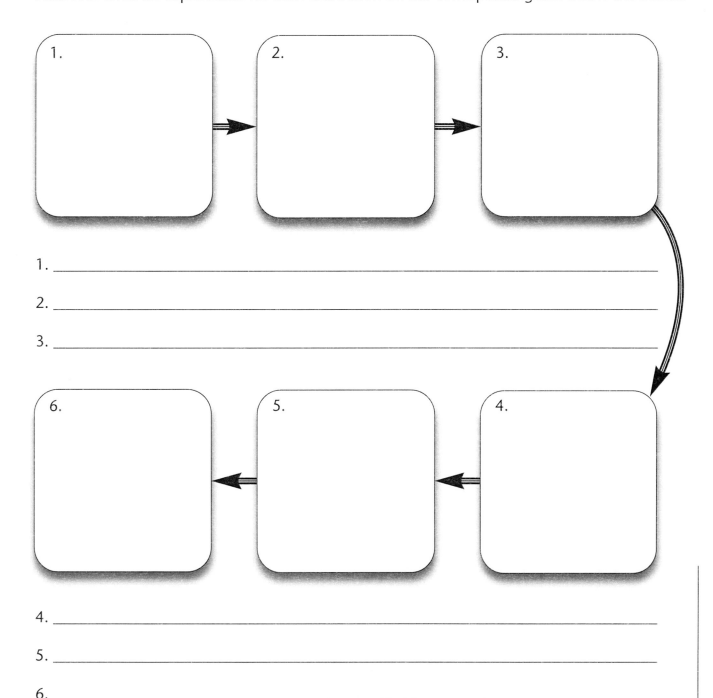

1. _____
2. _____
3. _____

4. _____
5. _____
6. _____

Sorting Characters

Directions: Similarities between characters are sometimes a clue to themes in a story. Place this novel's characters in one or more of the groups below.

Victims	Victimizers	Fighters

Peace-lovers	Conformists	Self-directors

Story Map

Directions: Complete the story map for *The Boy in the Striped Pajamas*.

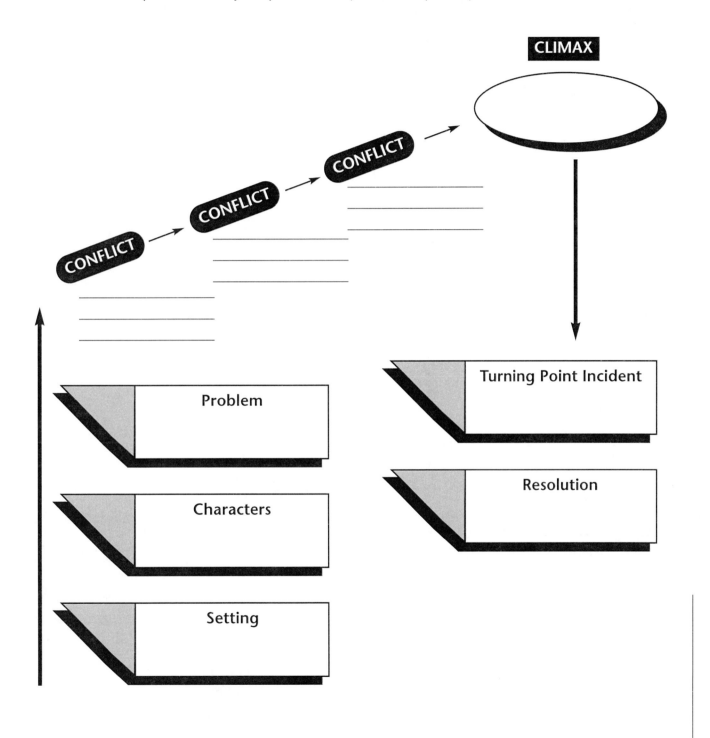

Character Web

Directions: Choose a character from the novel, and complete the chart below. Cite evidence from the story as you fill in information.

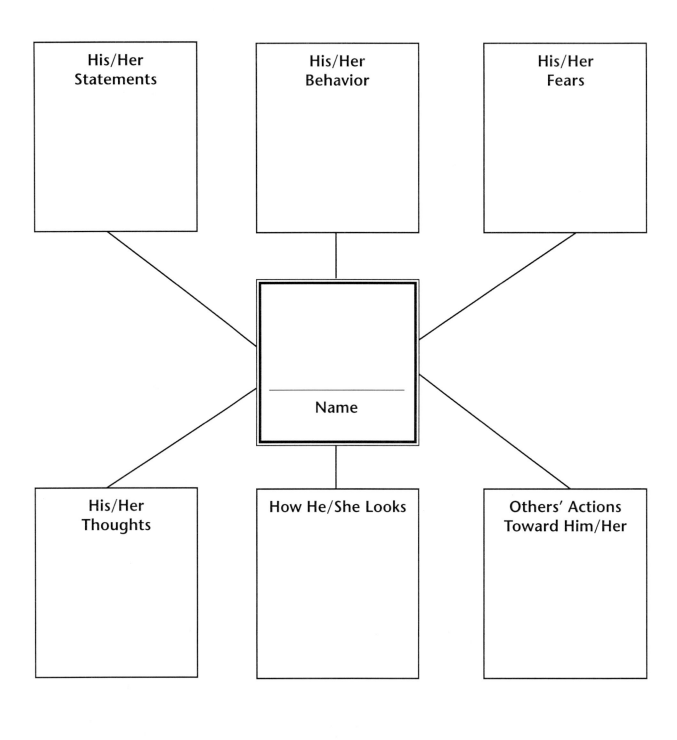

Cause/Effect

Directions: To plot cause and effect in a story, first list the sequence of events. Then mark causes with a C and effects with an E. Sometimes in a chain of events, one item may be both a cause and an effect. Draw arrows from cause statements to the appropriate effects.

Events in the story	Cause	Effect
1.		
2.		
3.		
4.		
5.		
6.		
7.		
8.		
9.		
10.		

Another way to map cause and effect is to look for an effect and then backtrack to the single or multiple causes.

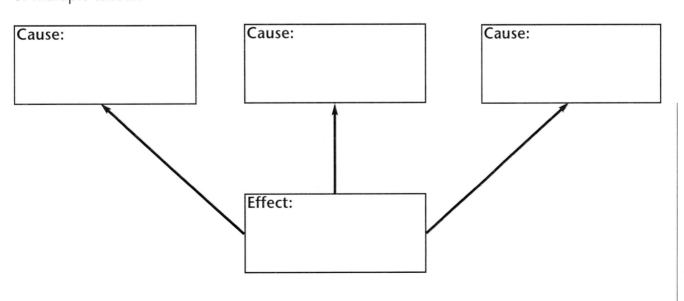

Linking Novel Units® Lessons to National and State Reading Assessments

During the past several years, an increasing number of students have faced some form of state-mandated competency testing in reading. Many states now administer state-developed assessments to measure the skills and knowledge emphasized in their particular reading curriculum. The discussion questions and post-reading questions in this Novel Units® Teacher Guide make excellent open-ended comprehension questions and may be used throughout the daily lessons as practice activities. The rubric below provides important information for evaluating responses to open-ended comprehension questions. Teachers may also use scoring rubrics provided for their own state's competency test.

Please note: The Novel Units® Student Packet contains optional open-ended questions in a format similar to many national and state reading assessments.

Scoring Rubric for Open-Ended Items

3-Exemplary	Thorough, complete ideas/information Clear organization throughout Logical reasoning/conclusions Thorough understanding of reading task Accurate, complete response
2-Sufficient	Many relevant ideas/pieces of information Clear organization throughout most of response Minor problems in logical reasoning/conclusions General understanding of reading task Generally accurate and complete response
1-Partially Sufficient	Minimally relevant ideas/information Obvious gaps in organization Obvious problems in logical reasoning/conclusions Minimal understanding of reading task Inaccuracies/incomplete response
0-Insufficient	Irrelevant ideas/information No coherent organization Major problems in logical reasoning/conclusions Little or no understanding of reading task Generally inaccurate/incomplete response